Carol, gaily carol

Christm

choser

CW00495194

with PIANO accompaniments,
with chords for GUITAR, and with parts
for descant recorders, glockenspiel, chime bars
and percussion

A & C Black · London

Published by A & C Black (Publishers) Limited   35 Bedford Row   London WC1R 4JH   © 1980, 1975 A & C Black Ltd
First published 1973.   Reprinted 1974 (twice), 1975, 1978, 1980 (with additional material), 1982, 1984, 1987

ISBN 0-7136-1872-8
Printed in Great Britain by Hollen Street Press Ltd at Slough, Berkshire

Contents

Shepherds and kings

Celebrating Christmas

Notes on the music

Piano accompaniments

These are provided for all tunes and have been kept as simple as possible.

Descant recorder/glockenspiel

The following tunes have additional parts for these instruments:
1, 5, 6, 8, 10, 23, 27, 31, 33, 39.

Chime bars

Parts for chime bars, using in general only one, two or three notes, are given for the following tunes:
6, 13, 19, 33, 34, 42.

Percussion instruments

Varied percussion accompaniments are suggested for the following tunes. These are by no means exhaustive and many others will suggest themselves.
2, 3, 4, 6, 7, 9, 11, 12, 13, 14, 15, 19, 21, 24, 25, 26, 27, 28, 29, 30, 36, 37, 38, 40, 41.

Guitar chords

Guitar chords are suggested for all tunes. All the chords you will need are given below. A cross above a string means that it should not be sounded. A bracket linking two or more strings indicates that they should be held down simultaneously by the first finger.

A
A⁷
Am
Am7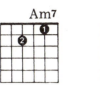
A⁹
B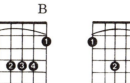
B⁷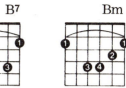
Bm
Bm7

B♭
B♭⁷
B♭ maj⁷
C
C⁷
3rd fret x C⁷sus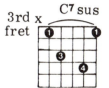
3rd fret Cm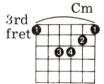

x D
x D⁷
x Dm
x Dm7
E
E⁷
Em
Em7

F
F⁷
x F maj⁷
G
G⁷
Gmaj7
Gm
Gm7

1 Mary met an angel

1 Mary met an angel unexpectedly,
   When she was a-walking in the garden.
   Mary said, "Oh angel, how you startled me!"
   When she was a-walking in the garden.

2 Mary was excited and fell on her knee,
   When she met the angel in the garden.
   Angel he said, "Mary, don't be scared of me,"
   When she met that angel in the garden.

3 Angel promised Mary God would send a son,
   As they stood there talking in the garden.
   "When he comes," he said, "he'll be a special
       one,"
   As they stood there talking in the garden.

4 Angel disappeared unexpectedly;
   Mary went on walking in the garden.
   She thought, "It's quite marvellous that God
       chose me,"
   As she went on walking in the garden.

Words: Peggy Blakeley
Music: Don Harper

gar - den. _____ Ma - ry said, "Oh

Gm7   C7   F7

an - gel, how you start - led me!"

F7   Bb

When she was a - walk · ing in the gar - den. _____

F   Dm7   G7   C7(sus4)   F

2 Now tell us, gentle Mary

1 Now tell us, gentle Mary,
   What did Gabriel say to you?
   Now tell us of the tidings
   That he brought to Galilee.
   He told me I was favoured,
   That I would be the one
   God chose to be the mother
   Of Jesus, his own son.

2 Now tell us, gentle Mary,
   Of the birth of Christ that morn.
   Now tell us of Christ Jesus,
   Where it was that he was born.
   Not in a palace glorious,
   Not in a silken bed,
   But in a stable humble
   Did Jesus lay his head.

Words: translated from the French by W. B. Lindsay
This version by Ruth Heller
Music: French traditional carol

fa - voured, That I would be the one God

Gm   Cm   D *tacit.*

chose to be the mo - ther Of Je - sus, his own son.

D   Gm   D   Gm

The triangles maintain a steady three beats in each bar throughout. The clash of the cymbal on the second beat of bars 4, 8 and 16 will accentuate the musical and vocal phrasing.

3 Little donkey

Little donkey, little donkey,
On the dusty road,
Got to keep on plodding onwards
With your precious load.
Been a long time, little donkey,
Through the winter's night.
Don't give up now, little donkey,
Bethlehem's in sight.

Ring out those bells tonight,
Bethlehem, Bethlehem.
Follow that star tonight,
Bethlehem, Bethlehem.
Little donkey, little donkey,
Had a heavy day.
Little donkey, carry Mary
Safely on her way.

Little donkey, carry Mary
Safely on her way.

Words and music: Eric Boswell
Piano accompaniment: G. C. Westcott

The following percussion accompaniment is suggested for this song:

Bars 1–16 (first four lines of music)

Use a gong drum to maintain a steady two beats in each bar throughout. From bar 4, use castanets or coconut shells to maintain the following bass rhythm to the end of bar 16:

Bars 17–24 (first eight bars on this page)

Use sleigh bells or wrist jingles, following the rhythm of the melody.

Bar 25 to end (from "Little donkey")

Gong drum and castanets or coconut shells take up the same two rhythms as in the first part and repeat them to the end.

4 Here we go up to Bethlehem

1 Here we go up to Bethlehem,
   Bethlehem, Bethlehem,
  Here we go up to Bethlehem
  On a cold and frosty morning.

2 We've got to be taxed in Bethlehem,
   Bethlehem, Bethlehem,
  We've got to be taxed in Bethlehem
  On a cold and frosty morning.

3 Where shall we stay in Bethlehem,
   Bethlehem, Bethlehem?
  Where shall we stay in Bethlehem
  On a cold and frosty morning?

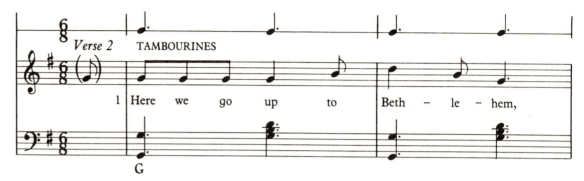

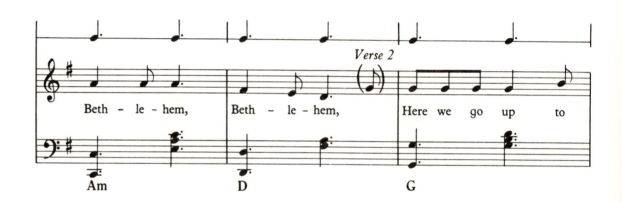

The children might add to the existing verses.

The method of playing the tambourines for the percussion accompaniment might be varied between tapping in the conventional way with the fingers, tapping on other parts of the body, shaking the instrument, or scratching with the finger nails, using a circular movement.

Words: Sydney Carter
Music: English traditional melody

5 Joseph is sad as he travels the way

1   Joseph is sad as he travels the way,
      Mary is tired at the end of the day.
      "Innkeeper, have you a room for us, pray?
      May we stay here till the morning?"

2   Here in the stable the weary may rest.
      Oxen and asses will welcome the guest,
      He will be safe as a bird in its nest,
      Jesus will come in the morning.

Words and music: E. M. Ponting
Piano arrangement: Percy M. Young

6 Lodging, I beg you, good man

1 Lodging, I beg you, good man,
  In the name of heaven!
  My wife is weary;
  She says she can go no farther.
  Long have we travelled,
  Have mercy on us, good man!
  God will reward you
  If you will give shelter to her.

2 There is no room in this place
  For any stranger.
  I do not know you;
  Be gone, and all talking cease!
  I do not care
  If great distance you have come.
  All of your pleading is vain,
  So go away, let us have our peace.

Words and melody: Mexican traditional carol, arranged by Ruth Heller.
Piano accompaniment: B.H.

Long have we tra-velled, Have mer-cy on us, good man!

D7   G

God will re-ward you If you will give shel-ter to her.

D   A7   D

As an alternative to descant recorder and chime bars, a simple percussion accompaniment such as the following might be used:

1st verse: Triangles marking the first beat of each bar or following the rhythm of the melody.

2nd verse: A gong drum or tambour and beater played loudly on the first beat of each bar.

7 Standing in the rain

Standing in the rain,
Knocking on the window,
Knocking on the window
On a Christmas Day.
There he is again,
Knocking on the window,
Knocking on the window
In the same old way.

1   No use knocking on the window.
    There is nothing we can do, sir.
    All the beds are booked already,
    There is nothing left for you, sir.
        Standing in the rain . . .

2   No, we haven't got a manger,
    No, we haven't got a stable.
    'Till you woke us with your knocking,
    We were sleeping like the dead, sir.
        Standing in the rain . . .

Words and music: Sydney Carter

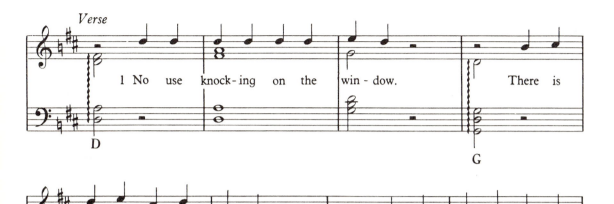

1 No use knock-ing on the win-dow. There is

D   G

no-thing we can do, sir. All the beds are booked al-

D

-rea-dy, There is no-thing left for you, sir.

A7   Dm   D.C.

The following percussion rhythm might be used throughout the chorus:

This could be played on a snare drum or bongo drum, or by knocking with the fist on a hollow building block.

8 There isn't any room

1   Rat-a-tat-tat, Rat-a-tat-tat,

     No! No! No!

     There isn't any room

     And you can't stay here,

     There isn't any room for strangers.

     The wind may be chill

     And the night may be cold,

     And be full of nasty noises in the dark

         and dangers.

     But there isn't any room,

         There isn't any room,

         There isn't any room for strangers.

2   Rat-a-tat-tat, Rat-a-tat-tat,

     Yes! Yes! Yes!

     There is a little room

     And you may stay here,

     We have a little place for strangers.

     Come in from the night

     To the stable so bare

     Which is full of warmth and friendliness

         and safe from dangers.

     Yes, there is a little room,

         There is a little room,

         There is a little room for strangers.

Words: Peggy Blakeley
Music: Don Harper

wind may be chill And the night may be cold, And be full of nas – ty

G   G7   C   G   A7

noi – ses in the dark and dan – gers. But there is – n't a – ny room, There

A9   Am7 D7   G

Bell (or D chime bar)

is – n't a – ny room, There is – n't a – ny room for stran – gers.

A7   Em7   Am7   D7   G

9 Baby Jesus, sleeping softly

1 Baby Jesus, sleeping softly
On the warm and fragrant hay,
Children all the wide world over
Think of you on Christmas Day.

2 Mother Mary watching Jesus
Sleeping in the soft warm hay,
Children all the wide world over
Think of you on Christmas Day.

3 Joseph standing close beside them
Hearing what the shepherds say,
Children all the wide world over
Think of you on Christmas Day.

One suggestion for percussion accompaniment is for chime bar F to be played on the first beat of each of the first four bars and then for triangles to follow the rhythm of the melody in the last four bars.

The children might try singing the first four bars unaccompanied except for the chime bar, the triangles and piano accompanying the second half of the tune.

(N.B. Chime bar F should not be used with the guitar chords suggested here.)

Words and music: Hilda M. Dodd

10 Come, see this little stranger

1 Come, see this little stranger
   That lies all warm within;
   His cradle is a manger,
   His home a way-side inn;
   Come, let us look within.

2 The breath of oxen warms him,
   They watch this baby dear,
   They see no chill shall harm him,
   So long as they are near,
   This little babe to cheer.

The descant recorder part may also be used as a second part for voices.

Words: J. Steuart Wilson
Music: G. C. Westcott
Name of tune: Denbridge

DESCANT RECORDER
Gently

1 Come, see this lit - tle stran - ger That lies all warm with -

(D) A7 D G

- in; His cra - dle is a man - ger, His

D A7 D

home a way - side inn; Come, let us look with - in.

G B7 Em A7 D

11 Come, they told me, parum pum pum pum

1 Come, they told me,
  parum pum pum pum,
A new-born king to see,
  parum pum pum pum,
Our finest gifts we bring,
  parum pum pum pum,
To lay before the king,
  parum pum pum pum,
  rum pum pum pum, rum pum pum pum.
So to honour him,
  parum pum pum pum,
When we come.

2 Baby Jesus . . .
  I am a poor boy too . . .
  I have no gift to bring . . .
  That's fit to give our king . . .
  Shall I play for you . . .
  On my drum?

3 Mary nodded . . .
  The ox and lamb kept time . . .
  I played my drum for him . . .
  I played my best for him . . .
  Then he smiled at me . . .
  Me and my drum.

Words: Katherine K. Davis
Music: Czech carol tune arranged by Harry Simeone and Henry Onorati
Title: The Little Drummer Boy

To lay be - fore the king, pa - rum pum pum pum,

F   Bb   F7   Bb

rum pum pum pum,   rum pum pum pum.

F   C

So   to   hon - our him, par - um pum pum pum,___

F   C7   F

when we come.___

Verses 1 and 2   Last time

C7   F

Drums can beat a steady two beats per bar throughout. The small notes marking the main beats above bars 6, 10, 14, 20, 24 and 26 can be played by a C chime bar.

12 Girls and boys, leave your toys

1 Girls and boys, leave your toys,
  make no noise,
Kneel at his crib and worship him.
At thy shrine, Child divine,
  we are thine,
Our Saviour's here.

  "Hallelujah" the church bells ring,
  "Hallelujah" the angels sing,
  "Hallelujah" from everything.
  All must draw near.

2 On that day, far away,
  Jesus lay,
Angels were watching round his head.
Holy child, mother mild,
  undefiled,
We sing thy praise.
  "Hallelujah" the church bells ring ...

3 Shepherds came at the fame
  of thy name,
Angels their guide to Bethlehem.
In that place, saw thy face
  filled with grace,
Stood at thy door.
  "Hallelujah" the church bells ring ...

Words: Malcolm Sargent
Music: Czech folk tune
Piano accompaniment: B.H.

CYMBALS, TRIANGLES AND TAMBOURINES

"Hal - le - lu – jah" the church bells ring,

G   D

"Hal - le - lu – jah" the an - gels sing, "Hal - le - lu – jah" from

A7   D   Em

ev - ery - thing. All must draw near.

Bm7   A7   D

13 Hey, little bull behind the gate

Hey, little bull behind the gate,
What are you doing up so late?
And, little bull, what have you seen
On this starry Christmas Eve?

1 If you raise your eyes to heaven
You will see the Virgin's Son,
He is clothed in white apparel
And is blessing everyone.

La-la la-la la la la la la
La la la la-la la-la la-la la
La-la la-la la la la la la
La la-la la la-la la la la.

2 Forward, forward, little shepherd,
March on bravely, everyone,
Thanking God with hearts o'erflowing
For the gift of his blessed son.

Hey, little bull behind the gate,
What are you doing up so late?
And, little bull, what have you seen
On this starry Christmas Eve?

Words: English words by A. H. Green
Music: Latin-American carol tune
Piano accompaniment: G. C. Westcott

He is clothed in white ap-par-el And is bless-ing ev-ery-one.

A7   D   A7   D

Chorus 2

La-la la-la la la   la   la   la   La   la   la   la-la   la-la la-la la

D   G   D   G   D   A7   D

La-la la-la la la   la   la   la   La   la-la   la   la-la   la   la   la.

G   D   G   D   A7   D

The part for chime bars uses only D, G and A.

A percussion accompaniment to this carol might be provided by triangles and drums as follows:

Choruses 1 and 3

Triangles play the rhythm of the melody.

Verses 1 and 2 and chorus 2

Drums play two minim beats in each bar.

The children might like to make up their own words for the verses.

14 Infant holy, infant lowly

1 Infant holy, infant lowly,
   For his bed a cattle stall;
   Oxen lowing, little knowing
   Christ the babe is Lord of all.
   Swift are winging angels singing,
   Nowell's ringing, tidings bringing,
   Christ the babe is Lord of all,
   Christ the babe is Lord of all.

2 Flocks were sleeping, shepherds keeping
   Vigil till the morning new,
   Saw the glory, heard the story,
   Tidings of a gospel true.
   Thus rejoicing, free from sorrow,
   Praises voicing, greet the morrow,
   Christ the babe was born for you,
   Christ the babe was born for you.

As an additional percussion accompaniment, drums might beat
the following rhythm throughout:

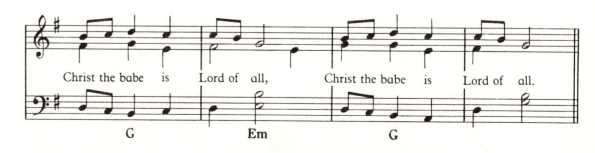

Words: E. M. G. Reed
Music: Polish carol melody

15 It was poor little Jesus

1   It was poor little Jesus,
      Yes, Yes.
He was born on a Friday,
      Yes, Yes.
Didn't have no cradle,
      Yes, Yes.

    Wasn't that a pity and a shame,
    O Lord.
    Wasn't that a pity and a shame.

2   It was poor little Jesus,
      Yes, Yes.
The child of Mary,
      Yes, Yes.
He was laid in a manger,
      Yes, Yes.
    Wasn't that a pity . . .

3   He was born on a Christmas,
      Yes, Yes.
He was born on a Christmas,
      Yes, Yes.
Didn't have no shelter,
      Yes, Yes.
    Wasn't that a pity . . .

Drums might beat the following rhythm throughout:

Words and music: American spiritual
Piano accompaniment: G. C. Westcott

16 Jesus, Jesus, rest your head

Jesus, Jesus, rest your head,
You has got a manger bed.
All the evil folk on earth
Sleep in feathers at their birth.
Jesus, Jesus, rest your head,
You has got a manger bed.

1 Have you heard about our Jesus?
Have you heard about his fate?
How his mammy went to that stable
On that Christmas Eve so late?
Winds were blowing, cows were lowing,
Stars were glowing, glowing, glowing.
     Jesus, Jesus, rest your head ...

2 To that manger came the wise men,
Bringing things from hin and yon
For the mother and the father
And the blessed little son.
Milkmaids left their fields and flocks
And sat beside the ass and ox.
     Jesus, Jesus, rest your head ...

Words and music: American folk song, collected by John Jacob Niles
Piano accompaniment: B.H.

Verse

1 Have you heard a-bout our Je-sus? Have you heard a-

Bm   G

-bout his fate? How his mam-my went to that sta-ble

A   Bm   D

On that Christ-mas Eve so late? Winds were blow-ing,

G   A   Bm   G

D.C.

cows were low-ing, Stars were glow-ing, glow-ing, glow-ing.

D   A   Gmaj7   A7

17 Jesus borned in Bethlea

Jesus borned in Bethlea,
Jesus borned in Bethlea,
Jesus borned in Bethlea,
    and in the manger lay.
And in the manger lay,
    and in the manger lay,
Jesus borned in Bethlea,
    and in the manger lay.

The children might make up additional verses to this carol, basing them on the Christmas story. Only two unrhymed lines are needed.

Words and music: American folk song, collected by
   Sidney Robertson

18 Jesus, our brother, kind and good

FIRST TUNE

1 Jesus, our brother, kind and good,
   Was humbly born in a stable rude;
   And the friendly beasts around him stood,
   Jesus, our brother, kind and good.

2 "I," said the donkey, shaggy and brown,
   "I carried his mother up-hill and down,
   I carried her safely to Bethlehem town."
   "I," said the donkey, shaggy and brown.

3 "I," said the cow, all white and red,
   "I gave him my manger for a bed,
   I gave him my hay to pillow his head."
   "I," said the cow, all white and red.

4 "I," said the sheep with the curly horn,
   "I gave him my wool for a blanket warm,
   He wore my coat on Christmas morn."
   "I," said the sheep with the curly horn.

5 "I," said the dove from the rafters high,
   "I cooed him to sleep so he would not cry,
   We cooed him to sleep, my mate and I."
   "I," said the dove from the rafters high.

   Repeat the first verse

Words and music: English traditional carol

A second tune is given on the next page

18 Jesus, our brother, kind and good

1 Jesus, our brother, kind and good,
Was humbly born in a stable rude;
And the friendly beasts around him stood,
Jesus, our brother, kind and good.

2 "I," said the donkey, shaggy and brown,
"I carried his mother up-hill and down,
I carried her safely to Bethlehem town."
"I," said the donkey, shaggy and brown.

3 "I," said the cow, all white and red,
"I gave him my manger for a bed,
I gave him my hay to pillow his head."
"I," said the cow, all white and red.

4 "I," said the sheep with the curly horn,
"I gave him my wool for a blanket warm,
He wore my coat on Christmas morn."
"I," said the sheep with the curly horn.

5 "I," said the dove from the rafters high,
"I cooed him to sleep so he would not cry,
We cooed him to sleep, my mate and I."
"I," said the dove from the rafters high.

Repeat the first verse

Words: English traditional carol
Music: G. C. Westcott
Name of tune: Staughton 2

SECOND TUNE

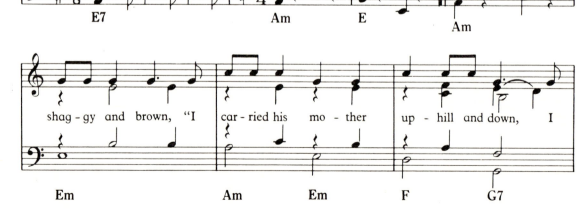

19 Lullaby, Jesus, my dear one, be sleeping

1 Lullaby, Jesus,
  My dear one, be sleeping.
  Lullaby, Jesus,
  While watch I am keeping.

    Lullaby, baby,
    My darling, I love you.
    Your mother will sing
    And so gently will rock you.

2 When you awaken,
  Sweet Jesus, I'll give you
  Raisins and almonds
  And sweet berries too.
    Lullaby, baby . . .

3 Hush, he is sleeping
  While stars shine above us;
  Like the bright sun
  Is the sweet baby Jesus.
    Lullaby, baby . . .

Words and music : Polish traditional carol,
  arranged by Haig and Regina Shekerjian

The rhythm of the chime bars part changes in the chorus to give a different pulse.

Any of the rhythms from the carol might be used as a recurring theme, to be played on triangles or tambourines. The rhythms included in this carol, with the number of the bar in which they occur, are:

Bar 2

Bar 3

Bar 4

Bar 10

Bar 1

Bar 7

20 A little child was born in a stall

1 A little child was born in a stall,
   A little child was born in a stall.
   He brought to the world much joy for us all,
   He brought to the world much joy for us all.

2 Yes, God's own son in a manger lay,
   Yes, God's own son in a manger lay.
   He slept in a cradle of wood and of hay,
   He slept in a cradle of wood and of hay.

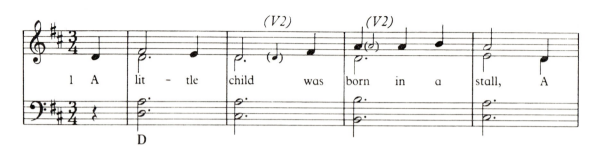

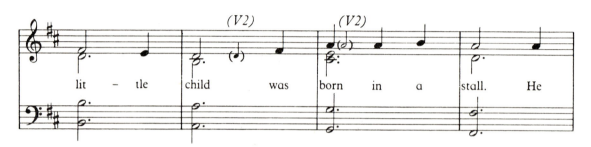

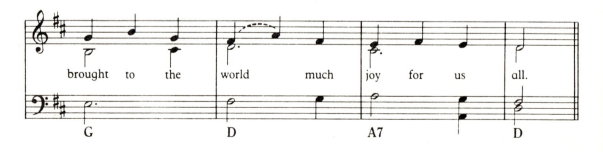

Words and music: from a Netherlands carol

21 Mary had a baby

1   Mary had a baby,
        Yes, Lord.
     Mary had a baby,
        Yes, my Lord.
     Mary had a baby,
        Yes, Lord.
        The people keep a-coming
        And the train done gone.

2   What did she name him?
        Yes, Lord . . .

3   Mary named him Jesus,
        Yes, Lord . . .

4   Where was he born?
        Yes, Lord . . .

5   Born in a stable,
        Yes, Lord . . .

6   Where did Mary lay him?
        Yes, Lord . . .

7   Laid him in a manger,
        Yes, Lord . . .

The children can add to the existing verses, building up the Christmas story.

As a percussion accompaniment, a gong drum and beater is suggested, playing two beats in each bar.

Words and music: St. Helena Island spiritual

22 Mary was watching tenderly

1   Mary was watching tenderly
        Her little son;
    Softly the mother sang to sleep
        Her darling one.
    Sleep, lovely child, be now at rest,
        Dear son of light;
    Sleep, pretty fledgling, in your nest
        All through the night.

2   Mary has spread your manger bed,
        Sleep, little dove;
    God's creatures all draw near to praise
        And give their love.
    Sleep little pearl, creator, Lord,
        Our praises take;
    Bees bring you honey from their hoard
        When you awake.

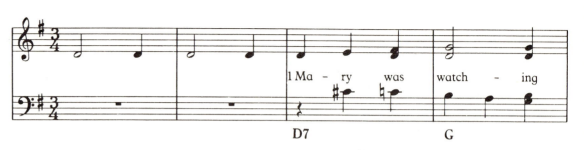

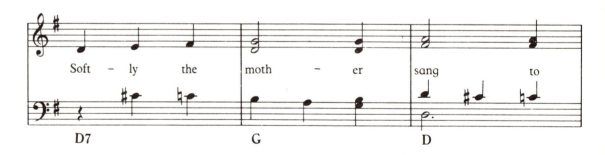

Words: translated from the Czech by M. C. Vojacek
Music: Czech traditional melody

Sleep, love - ly child, be now at

G

rest, Dear son of light;

D   A7   D

Sleep, pret - ty fledg - ling, in your

G   Em

nest All through the night.

D   D7   G

23 O come, little children

1 O come, little children,
    O come, one and all!
O come to the cradle
    in Bethlehem's stall;
The bright star will guide us
    and show us the way
To Jesus who's lying
    asleep on the hay.

2 O come, everybody,
    O come to the stall,
With hearts full of love
    for this baby so small.
O sing, little children,
    to him you adore;
O sing with the angels,
    sing peace evermore!

Words: Christoph von Schmid
Music: Johann A. P. Schulz

DESCANT RECORDER OR GLOCKENSPIEL

The descant recorder part may also be used as a second part for voices.

guide   us   and   show   us   the   way   To

D   G

Je - sus who's ly — ing a - sleep on the hay.

A7   D   A7   D